AIR FRYER COOKBOOK Mastery 2021

50 EASY AND MOUTHWATERING RECIPES

TO ENJOY ALL THE BENEFITS OF AIR FRYING

Juliana Davis

TABLE OF CONTENTS

Introduction 9

Breakfast 12

    Cauliflower and Avocado Toast 12

    Fennel Frittata 14

    Silken Tofu Morning Treat 16

    Mixed Vegetable Frittata 18

    Peanut Oats and Chia Porridge 21

    Nutmeg Cranberry Scones 23

    Egg and Ham Cups 25

    Breakfast Stuffed Poblanos 27

    Bell Pepper Eggs 29

    Mixed Berries Oatmeal 31

Snacks , Sides and Appetizers 34

    Green Bean Crisps 34

    Cajun Fried Green Tomatoes 36

    Salmon Croquettes 38

    Parmesan Onion Rings 40

    Olive and Calamari Rings 42

    Air Fried Leeks 43

    Fried Pickles 44

Spring Onion and Tuna Salad...46

Feta Cheese Dip...47

White Onion and Sweet Potato Mix..................................48

Lunch...50

Pumpkin Lasagna..50

Rustic Baked Halloumi with Fennel Salad.......................53

Five Spicy Crispy Roasted Pork...55

Tuscan Pork Chops...56

Thai Basil Pork...58

Creamy Herbed Turkey...60

Chicken Bruschetta..62

Juicy & Spicy Chicken Wings..64

Air-fried Green Herbs Scallop..65

Mustard Tuna Cakes..67

Dinner..69

Rosemary Veggie Gratin...69

Vegan Sausages...71

Spicy Short Ribs in Red Wine Reduction.........................73

Coffee Rubbed Steaks...75

Creamy Cajun Chicken..77

Turkey with Mushrooms and Peas Casserole.................79

Thyme Chicken Balls..81

Ranch Fish Fillet 83

Herbed Fish Fingers 85

Quick and Easy Lobster Tails 88

Desserts 90

Fruit Custard 90

Beet Root Pudding 91

Lemon Poppy Muffins 93

Caramel Muffins 95

Cinnamon Churros 97

Chocolate Oatmeal Cookies 99

Cashew Cookies 101

Pears and Espresso Cream 103

Blackberry Cream Cheese Mousse 105

Hazelnut Spread 107

Conclusion 109

Introduction

Your tongue may have an affection for crispy fried food. But the arteries of yours? Not really. Excessive consumption of fried foods may lead to many diseases.

An air fryer is not just a regular fryer. It's like an oven fryer; it doesn't cook food as pan-frying or deep-frying would. It's essentially a small convection oven with a hot air chamber. It cooks the food a little quicker, spreads heat more equally in the perforated basket in which food is placed. Air fryer speeds up the cooking process, when one is in a hurry and needs to cook a delicious, healthy meal, to save you from all the trouble of waiting, there is an air fryer. The term fry always comes up with deep frying because they get food crispy while frying them and the opposite mechanism is with air fryers because they're not traditional fryers, and oil is not used to get the food crisp and healthy.

It is one of the healthiest methods to cook crispy and fried food. You can cook anything from baked seeds to moist cakes and everything in between. Air fryers are popular because they can give the food the fried crispiness without frying them at all, which is healthier than any fried foods but equally delicious or more.

In around 2013, air fryers first entered the market and now have become the kitchens' sensation. They will offer a crisp outer shell to your favorite foods without submerging them in oil. Think about Healthier French fries; although these terms do not go together, it is possible now, and the reason is cooking in the air fryer. Cooking on a sheet pan will give an equal performance, but it turns out the air fryer is quick, simple, and handy. So when baking, roasting in the oven becomes too much work give your time to air fryer; they will not let you down. Cooking with Air fryer on every standard is easier than frying in oil. It decreases calories by 70-80% and has less fat. Any of the other adverse consequences of oil frying may also be minimized by this form of cooking. That eventually allows the appetite for fried food a cooler and healthier option. The potential of air fryers to cook and reheat leftovers is remarkable. Foods such as arancini egg rolls, and taquitos, look as amazing as they tasted when they are made fresh. So, let's get started with delicious healthy, and affordable air fryer recipes.

Benefits of Air Frying Compared to Normal Frying

Food is healthier because oil use is greatly reduced. Still, everything comes out crispy and brown that is supposed to.

Food cooks quicker and more efficiently. Heat does not escape from the air fryer as it does on a cooktop or oven.

It takes less time to cook or reheat food because it stays in the air fryer and circulates.

The air fryer is more efficient. Because the heat stays in the unit and does not vent, it cooks more efficiently and faster without using as much electricity. I hate turning my oven on in the summer because it heats the house.

It is versatile, and you can make a variety of foods ranging from breakfast items to mouth-watering desserts.

Most units are small and fit on the countertop or in a cupboard for storage.

They are quite easy to clean, with lots of detachable parts and components that can be placed in the dishwasher.

Heating up frozen foods that would normally go in an oven at a high temperature can be cooked in a matter of minutes, including chicken tenders and nuggets, fish sticks, and frozen fries.

Breakfast

Cauliflower and Avocado Toast

Preparation Time: 15 minutes

Cooking Time: 10-15 minutes

Servings: 2

Ingredients:

¼ cup cauliflower

½ cup shredded mozzarella cheese

1 large egg.

1 ripe medium avocado

½ tsp. garlic powder.

¼ tsp. ground black pepper

Directions:

First, cook the cauliflower then remove the extra water by squeezing it out using a cheesecloth. Cook cauliflower according to package instructions. Now, mix in the mozzarella and egg with cauliflower in a bowl. Then, shape the cauliflower into two circles then put in the air fryer basket then cook. Make sure that halfway through cooking, flip the cauliflower.

Adjust the temperature to 400 Degrees F and set the timer for 8 minutes

Now the avocado must be slit open and scoop the flesh out, place it in a medium bowl and mash it with garlic powder and pepper. Spread onto the cauliflower.

Fennel Frittata

Preparation Time: 15 minutes

Cooking Time: 10-15 minutes

Servings: 6

Ingredients:

1 fennel bulb; shredded

6 eggs; whisked

2 tsp. cilantro; chopped.

1 tsp. sweet paprika

Cooking spray

A pinch of salt and black pepper

Directions:

Take a bowl and mix all the ingredients except the cooking spray and stir well.

Grease a baking pan with the cooking spray, pour the frittata mix and spread well

Put the pan in the Air Fryer and cook at 370°F for 15 minutes. Divide between plates and serve them for breakfast.

Silken Tofu Morning Treat

Preparation Time:5 minutes

Cooking Time: 10 minutes

Servings: 2

Ingredients:

½ teaspoon sesame oil

½ teaspoon olive oil

8-ounce silken tofu, pressed and made slices

3 eggs

2 teaspoons fish sauce

Black pepper as needed

1 teaspoon corn flour

2 teaspoons water

Directions:

Place your air fryer on a flat kitchen surface; plug it and turn it on. Set temperature to 390 degrees F and let it preheat for 4-5 minutes.

Take out the air-frying basket and gently coat it using a cooking oil or spray.

Add the tofu in the basket.

In a bowl of medium size, thoroughly whisk the corn flour into water.

In a bowl of large size, thoroughly mix the corn flour mixture, eggs, fish sauce, both oils, and pepper.

Add the eggs mixture over tofu.

Push the air-frying basket in the air fryer. Let your air fryer cook the added mixture for the next 10 minutes.

Slide out the basket; serve warm!

Mixed Vegetable Frittata

Preparation Time: 20 minutes

Cooking Time: 30 minutes

Servings: 6

Ingredients:

¼ cup milk

1 zucchini

½ bunch asparagus

½ cup mushrooms

½ cup spinach or baby spinach

½ cup red onion, sliced

4 eggs

½ tbsp. olive oil

5 tbsp. feta cheese, crumbled

4 tbsp. cheddar, grated

¼ bunch chives, minced

Sea salt and pepper to taste

Directions:

In a bowl, mix together the eggs, milk, salt and pepper.

Cut up the zucchini, asparagus, mushrooms and red onion into slices. Shred the spinach using your hands.

Over a medium heat, stir-fry the vegetables for 5 – 7 minutes with the olive oil in a non-stick pan.

Place some parchment paper in the base of a baking tin. Pour in the vegetables, followed by the egg mixture. Top with the feta and grated cheddar.

Set the Air Fryer at 320°F and allow to warm for five minutes.

Transfer the baking tin to the fryer and allow to cook for 15 minutes. Take care when removing the frittata from the Air Fryer and leave to cool for 5 minutes.

Top with the minced chives and serve.

Peanut Oats and Chia Porridge

Preparation Time: 10 minutes

Cooking Time: 5 minutes

Servings: 4

Ingredients:

4 cups milk

2 tbsp. peanut butter

2 cups oats

1 cup chia seeds

4 tbsp. honey

1 tbsp. butter, melted

Directions:

Pre-heat the Air Fryer to 390°F.

Put the peanut butter, honey, butter, and milk in a bowl and mix together using a whisk. Add in the oats and chia seeds and stir.

Transfer the mixture to a fryer-proof bowl that is small enough to fit inside the fryer and cook for 5 minutes. Give another stir before serving.

Nutmeg Cranberry Scones

Preparation Time: 5 minutes

Cooking Time: 10 minutes

Servings: 4

Ingredients:

1 cup of fresh cranberries

⅓ cup of sugar

One tablespoon of orange zest

¾ cup of half and half cream

2 cups of flour

¼ teaspoon of ground nutmeg

¼ teaspoon of salt

¼ cup of butter, chilled and diced

¼ cup of brown sugar

One tablespoon of baking powder

One egg

Directions:

Set an Air fryer to 365 degrees F for 10 minutes. Strain nutmeg, flour, baking powder, salt, and sugar in a bowl. Blend in the cream and egg. Fold in the orange zest and cranberries to form a smooth dough. Roll the dough and cut into scones. Place the scones on the cooking tray. Insert the cooking tray in the Air fryer when it displays "Add Food." Flip the sides when it shows "Turn Food." Remove from the oven when cooking time is complete. Serve warm.

Egg and Ham Cups

Preparation Time: 15 minutes

Cooking Time: 15 minutes

Servings: 2

Ingredients:

4 large eggs.

4: 1-oz. slices deli ham

½ cup shredded medium Cheddar cheese.

¼ cup diced green bell pepper.

2 tbsp. diced red bell pepper.

2 tbsp. diced white onion.

2 tbsp. full-fat sour cream.

Directions:

Place one slice of ham on the bottom of four baking cups.

Take a large bowl, whisk eggs with sour cream. Stir in green pepper, red pepper and onion

Pour the egg mixture into ham-lined baking cups. Top with Cheddar. Place cups into the air fryer basket. Adjust the temperature to 320 Degrees F and set the timer for 12 minutes or until the tops are browned. Serve warm.

Breakfast Stuffed Poblanos

Preparation Time: 30 minutes

Cooking Time: 15-20 minutes

Servings: 2

Ingredients:

½ lb. spicy ground pork breakfast sausage

4 large poblano peppers

4 large eggs.

½ cup full-fat sour cream.

4 oz. full-fat cream cheese

¼ cup diced tomatoes and green chiles, drained

8 tbsp. shredded pepper jack cheese

Directions:

On a heated pan, brown the sausage that has been grinded and let it cook until there's no more in pink in color, take it out and remove excess fat. Put in the eggs in the same pan, and cook it as scrambled eggs.

Place cooked sausage in a large bowl and fold in cream cheese. Mix in diced tomatoes and chiles. Gently fold in eggs

Cut a 4"–5" slit in the top of each poblano, removing the seeds and white membrane with a small knife. Separate the filling into four and spoon carefully into each pepper. Top each with 2 tbsp. pepper jack cheese

Place each pepper into the air fryer basket. Adjust the temperature to 350 Degrees F and set the timer for 15 minutes. The cheese is golden brown and peppers will be soft when the mixture is done. Now, serve it with sour cream on top.

Bell Pepper Eggs

Preparation Time: 20 minutes

Cooking Time: 15 minutes

Servings: 4

Ingredients:

4 medium green bell peppers

¼ medium onion; peeled and chopped

3 oz. cooked ham; chopped

8 large eggs.

1 cup mild Cheddar cheese

Directions:

Cut the tops off each bell pepper. Remove the seeds and the white membranes with a small knife. Place ham and onion into each pepper

Crack 2 eggs into each pepper. Top with ¼ cup cheese per pepper. Place into the air fryer basket

Adjust the temperature to 390 Degrees F and set the timer for 15 minutes. When fully cooked, peppers will be tender and eggs will be firm. Serve immediately.

Mixed Berries Oatmeal

Preparation Time: 10 minutes

Cooking Time: 30 minutes

Servings: 2

Ingredients:

½ cup milk

1 egg

1 teaspoon vanilla extract

3 tablespoon brown sugar

6 tablespoon oatmeal

1 pinch salt

1 oz blackberry

1 oz strawberry

1 oz raspberry

1 pinch ground cinnamon

1 teaspoon honey

1 teaspoon butter

Directions:

Crack the egg into the bowl and whisk it.

Add the salt, vanilla extract, and milk. Stir it carefully.

Then combine the oatmeal and ground cinnamon together. Add the brown sugar and stir it.

Combine the blackberries, strawberries, and raspberries in the bowl. Shake them little.

Put the oatmeal in the air fryer basket.

Then pour the egg mixture and add berries.

Preheat the air fryer to 370 F and cook the meal for 30 minutes.

When the oatmeal is cooked – add butter and honey.

Mix it up and serve.

Snacks , Sides and Appetizers

Green Bean Crisps

Preparation Time: 15 minutes

Cooking Time: 10 minutes

Servings: 4-6

Ingredients:

1 lb. green beans, trimmed

1 tbsp olive oil

1 tsp garlic powder

1 tsp onion powder

1 tsp paprika

Salt and black pepper to taste

Directions:

Preheat air fryer to 390 F. Grease the air fryer basket with cooking spray.

In a bowl, mix olive oil, garlic and onion powders, paprika, salt, and pepper. Coat the green beans in the mixture and place them in the air fryer basket. Air Fry for 10 minutes, shaking once. Serve warm.

Cajun Fried Green Tomatoes

Preparation Time: 15 minutes

Cooking Time: 10 minutes

Servings: 4

Ingredients:

8 green tomato slices

2 egg whites

½ cup flour

1 cup breadcrumbs

1 tsp cayenne pepper

½ tsp mustard powder

Salt and black pepper to taste

Directions:

Preheat air fryer to 390 F. Spray the air fryer basket with cooking spray.

In a bowl, beat egg whites with salt. In a separate bowl, mix flour, mustard powder, cayenne pepper, salt, and black pepper. Add the breadcrumbs to a third bowl. Dredge tomato slices in the flour mixture, then in egg whites, and finally in the breadcrumbs. Spray with cooking spray and arrange in the fryer's basket. Air Fry for 10 minutes, turning once halfway through cooking. Serve warm.

Salmon Croquettes

Preparation Time: 20 minutes

Cooking Time: 10-15 minutes

Servings: 4

Ingredients:

1 (15 oz) tinned salmon, flaked

1 cup onions, grated

1 ½ cups carrots, grated

3 large eggs

1 ½ tbsp fresh chives, chopped

4 tbsp mayonnaise

4 tbsp breadcrumbs

2 ½ tsp Italian seasoning

Salt and black pepper to taste

2 ½ tsp lemon juice

Directions:

In a bowl, add salmon, onion, carrots, eggs, chives, mayonnaise, crumbs, Italian seasoning, pepper, salt, and lemon juice, and mix well. Form croquettes out of the mixture and refrigerate for 45 minutes.

Preheat air fryer to 400 F and grease the basket with cooking spray. Arrange croquettes in a single layer in the basket and spray with cooking spray. Air Fry for 10-12 minutes, flipping once, until golden.

Parmesan Onion Rings

Preparation Time: 30 minutes

Cooking Time: 8-10 minutes

Servings: 2

Ingredients:

1 onion, peeled and sliced into 1-inch rings

¾ cup Parmesan cheese, shredded

2 medium eggs, beaten

1 tsp garlic powder

A pinch of salt

1 cup flour

1 tsp paprika powder

Directions:

Beat the eggs in a bowl. In another bowl, mix cheese, garlic powder, salt, flour, and paprika.

Dip onion rings in egg, then in the cheese mixture, in the egg again and finally in the cheese mixture.

Add the rings to the frying basket and Air Fry for 8 minutes at 350 F.

Serve with honey-mustard dipping sauce.

Olive and Calamari Rings

Preparation Time: 20 minutes

Cooking Time: 20-30 minutes

Servings: 4

Ingredients:

1 lb. calamari rings

2 tbsp cilantro, chopped

1 chili pepper, minced

2 tbsp olive oil

1 cup pimiento-stuffed green olives

Salt and black pepper to taste

Directions:

In a bowl, add calamari rings, chili pepper, salt, black pepper, olive oil, and fresh cilantro. Marinate for 10 minutes. Pour the calamari into a baking dish and place it inside the fryer. Air Fry for 15 minutes, stirring every 5 minutes at 400 F. Serve warm with pimiento-stuffed olives.

Air Fried Leeks

Preparation Time: 10 minutes

Cooking Time: 7 minutes

Servings: 2

Ingredients:

2 leeks, washed, ends cut, and halved

Salt and black pepper, to taste

½ tablespoon butter, melted

½ tablespoon lemon juice

Directions:

Rub leeks with melted butter and season with salt and pepper.

Lay it inside the air fryer and cook at 350F for 7 minutes.

Arrange on a platter. Drizzle with lemon juice and serve.

Fried Pickles

Preparation Time: 20 minutes

Cooking Time: 15 minutes

Servings: 4

Ingredients:

14 dill pickles, sliced

¼ cup flour

1/8 tsp. baking powder

Pinch of salt

2 tbsp. cornstarch + 3 tbsp. water

6 tbsp. bread crumbs

½ tsp. paprika

Cooking spray

Directions:

Pre-heat your Air Fryer at 400°F.

Drain any excess moisture out of the dill pickles on a paper towel.

In a bowl, combine the flour, baking powder and salt.

Throw in the cornstarch and water mixture and combine well with a whisk.

Put the panko bread crumbs in a shallow dish along with the paprika. Mix thoroughly.

Dip the pickles in the flour batter, before coating in the bread crumbs. Spritz all the pickles with the cooking spray.

Transfer to the fryer and cook for 15 minutes, until a golden-brown color is achieved.

Spring Onion and Tuna Salad

Preparation Time: 10 minutes

Cooking Time: 15 minutes

Servings: 2

Ingredients:

14 oz. canned tuna, drained and flaked

2 spring onions; chopped.

1 cup arugula

1 tbsp. olive oil

A pinch of salt and black pepper

Directions:

In a bowl, all the ingredients except the oil and the arugula and whisk.

Preheat the Air Fryer over 360°F, add the oil and grease it. Pour the tuna mix, stir well and cook for 15 minutes

In a salad bowl, combine the arugula with the tuna mix, toss and serve.

Feta Cheese Dip

Preparation Time: 5 minutes

Cooking Time: 5 minutes

Servings: 6

Ingredients:

2 avocados, peeled, pitted and mashed

¼ cup spring onion; chopped.

1 garlic clove; minced

¼ cup parsley; chopped.

½ cup feta cheese, crumbled

1 tbsp. jalapeno; minced

Juice of 1 lime

Directions:

In a ramekin, mix all the ingredients and whisk them well.

Introduce in the fryer and cook at 380°F for 5 minutes. Serve as a party dip right away

White Onion and Sweet Potato Mix

Preparation Time: 10 minutes

Cooking Time: 15 minutes

Servings: 4

Ingredients:

2 sweet potatoes, peeled

1 red onion, peeled

1 white onion, peeled

1 teaspoon olive oil

¼ cup almond milk

Directions:

Chop the sweet potatoes and the onions into cubes.

Sprinkle the sweet potatoes with olive oil.

Put sweet potatoes in the air fryer basket and cook for 5 minutes at 400° F.

Then stir the sweet potatoes and add the chopped onions.

Pour in the almond milk and stir gently.

Cook the mix for 10 minutes more at 400° F.

When the mix is cooked, let it cool a little and serve.

Lunch

Pumpkin Lasagna

Preparation Time: 20 minutes

Cooking Time: 60 minutes

Servings: 6

Ingredients:

28 oz. Pumpkin, cut into slices

1 bunch sage, chopped

1/2 cup ghee, melted

1 leek, thinly sliced

4 garlic cloves, finely grated

3.5 oz. Kale and cavolo nero leaves shredded

270g semi-dried tomatoes, drained, chopped

17 0z. Quark

2 eggs, lightly beaten

Directions:

Mix pumpkin slices with sage leaves, 2 teaspoon salt, 2 tablespoon ghee in a bowl.

Toss leek separately with 2 tablespoon ghee, garlic, and ½ teaspoon salt in another bowl.

Mix kale with 1 teaspoon salt, tomato, and cavolo nero in a bowl.

Now beat eggs with quark and sage in a bowl.

Take a baking pan that can fit into the air fryer duo.

Add 1/3 of the leek mixture at the base of the baking pan.

Top this mixture with a layer of pumpkin slices.

Add 1/3 of quark mixture on top then add 1/3 of kale mixture over it.

Top it with pumpkin slices and continue repeating the layer while ending at the pumpkin slice layer on top.

Place the baking pan in the air fryer duo.

Put on the air fryer lid and seal it.

Hit the "bake button" and select 60 minutes of cooking time, then press "start."

Once the air fryer duo beeps, remove its lid.

Serve.

Rustic Baked Halloumi with Fennel Salad

Preparation Time: 20 minutes

Cooking Time: 35 minutes

Servings: 4

Ingredients:

Olive oil, to brush

7 oz. Sweet potato, coarsely grated

10 oz. Potatoes, coarsely grated

10 oz. Carrots, coarsely grated

9 oz. Halloumi, coarsely grated

1/2 onion, coarsely grated

2 tbsp thyme leaves

2 eggs

1/3 cup plain flour

1/2 cup sour cream, to serve

Fennel salad

2 celery stalks, thinly sliced

1 fennel, thinly sliced

1/2 cup olives, chopped

Juice of 1 lemon

1 lemon quarter, chopped

1 teaspoon toasted coriander seeds, ground

Directions:

Toss sweet potato, carrot, potato, onion, halloumi, thyme, flour, and eggs in a bowl.

Spread this mixture in the air fryer duo insert.

Put on the air fryer lid and seal it.

Hit the "bake button" and select 35 minutes of cooking time, then press "start."

Once the air fryer duo beeps, remove its lid.

Prepare the salad by mixing its ingredients: in a salad bowl.

Serve the sweet potato rosti with the prepared salad.

Five Spicy Crispy Roasted Pork

Preparation Time: 20 minutes

Cooking Time: 35 minutes

Servings: 6

Ingredients:

1 teaspoon Chinese five spice powder

1 teaspoon white pepper

2 pounds pork belly

2 teaspoons garlic salt

Directions:

Preheat the air fryer oven to 390°f.

Mix all the spices in a bowl to create the dry rub.

Score the skin of the pork belly with a knife and season the entire pork with the spice rub.

Place in the air fryer basket and cook for 40 to 45 minutes until the skin is crispy.

Chop before serving.

Tuscan Pork Chops

Preparation Time: 20 minutes

Cooking Time: 10-15 minutes

Servings: 4

Ingredients:

1/4 cup all-purpose flour

1 teaspoon salt

3/4 teaspoons seasoned pepper

4 (1-inch-thick) boneless pork chops

1 tablespoon olive oil

3 to 4 garlic cloves

1/3 cup balsamic vinegar

1/3 cup chicken broth

3 plum tomatoes, seeded and diced

Tablespoons capers

Directions:

Combine flour, salt, and pepper

Press pork chops into flour mixture on both sides until evenly covered.

Cook in your air fryer oven at 360 degrees for 14 minutes, flipping halfway through.

While the pork chops cook, warm olive oil in a medium skillet.

Add garlic and sauté for 1 minute; then mix in vinegar and chicken broth.

Add capers and tomatoes and turn to high heat.

Bring the sauce to a boil, stirring regularly, then add pork chops, Cooking for one minute.

Remove from heat and cover for about 5 minutes to allow the pork to absorb some of the sauce; serve hot.

Thai Basil Pork

Preparation Time: 10 minutes

Cooking Time: 15 minutes

Servings: 4

Ingredients:

1 minced hot chili

1 minced shallot

1-pound ground pork

2 tablespoons fish sauce

2 tablespoons lime juice

3 tablespoons basil

Tablespoons chopped mint

3 tablespoons cilantro

Directions:

In a shallow dish, mix well all Ingredients with hands. Form into 1-inch ovals.

Thread ovals in skewers. Place on skewer rack in air fryer.

For 15 minutes, cook on 360°f. Halfway through Cooking time, turnover skewers. If needed, cook in batches.

Serve and enjoy.

Creamy Herbed Turkey

Preparation Time: 2 hrs.

Cooking Time: 23 minutes

Servings: 2

Ingredients:

1/3 cup sour cream

2 cloves garlic, finely minced

1/3 teaspoon lemon zest

2 small-sized turkey breasts, skinless and cubed

1/3 cup thickened cream

2 tablespoons lemon juice

1 teaspoon fresh marjoram, chopped

Salt and freshly cracked mixed peppercorns, to taste

1/2 cup scallion, chopped

1/2 can tomatoes, diced

1 ½ tablespoons canola oil

Directions:

Firstly, pat dry the turkey breast. Mix the remaining items; marinate the turkey for 2 hours.

Set the air fryer to cook at 355 degrees F. Brush the turkey with a nonstick spray; cook for 23 minutes, turning once. Serve with naan and enjoy!

Chicken Bruschetta

Preparation Time: 30 minutes

Cooking Time: 30 minutes

Servings: 4

Ingredients:

3 ripe tomatoes, cubed

2 minced cloves garlic

¼ c. chopped red onion

2 tbsps. chopped basil leaves

1 tbsp. balsamic vinegar

3 oz. diced mozzarella

8 thinly sliced chicken cutlets

1 tbsp. olive oil

Salt and ground black pepper

Directions:

Place cubed tomatoes in a bowl. Mix in balsamic, pepper, onion, basil olive oil and garlic. Set aside for 15-20 minutes to blend the flavors. Mix in the cheese when ready to serve.

Preheat your air fryer to 360 °F.

Apply black pepper and salt to the chicken.

Coat the air fryer basket with cooking spray.

Place the chicken cutlets in the basket and cook for 6 minutes, turning over halfway through the cooking time.

Transfer to a plate.

Top the cutlets with the tomato mixture and serve.

Juicy & Spicy Chicken Wings

Preparation Time: 10 minutes

Cooking Time: 30 minutes

Servings: 4

Ingredients:

2 lbs. chicken wings

12 oz hot sauce

1 tsp Worcestershire sauce

1 tsp Tabasco

6 tbsp butter, melted

Directions:

Spray air fryer basket with cooking spray.

Add chicken wings into the air fryer basket and cook at 380 F for 25 minutes. Shake basket after every 5 minutes.

Meanwhile, in a bowl, mix together hot sauce, Worcestershire sauce, and butter. Set aside.

Add chicken wings into the sauce and toss well.

Serve and enjoy.

Air-fried Green Herbs Scallop

Preparation Time: 5 minutes

Cooking Time: 10 minutes

Servings: 2

Ingredients:

2 tablespoon dried thyme

1 tablespoon dried oregano

2 teaspoons chipotle pepper

1 tablespoon ground coriander

1 tablespoon ground fennel

1-pound sea scallops, cleaned and patted dry

Black pepper (ground) and salt to taste

3 dried chilies

Directions:

In a mixing bowl, add scallops and other ingredients. Combine to mix well with each other.

Place Air fryer over kitchen platform. Place Air Fryer Lid on top. Press Air Fry, set the temperature to 375°F and set the timer to 5 minutes to preheat. Press "Start" and allow it to preheat for 5 minutes.

Take Air Fryer Basket, grease it with some cooking spray. In the basket, add scallops.

Place the basket in the inner pot of Air fryer, close Air Fryer Lid on top.

Press the "Air Fry" setting. Set temperature to 390°F and set the timer to 10 minutes. Press "Start."

Open Air Fryer Lid after cooking time is over. Serve warm.

Mustard Tuna Cakes

Preparation Time: 10 minutes

Cooking Time: 6 minutes

Servings: 4

Ingredients:

¼ cup breadcrumbs

1 tablespoon mustard

7 ounces of canned tuna

1 egg, large

¼ teaspoon salt

½ teaspoon ground black pepper

Directions:

In a mixing bowl, add the egg, tuna, bread crumbs, pepper, salt, and mustard. Combine the ingredients to mix well with each other. Prepare 4 patties from the mixture.

Grease Air Fryer Basket with some cooking spray. Add the patties.

Place Air fryer Air Fryer Crisp over kitchen platform. Press Air Fry, set the temperature to 400°F and set the timer to 5 minutes to preheat. Press "Start" and allow it to pre-heat for 5 minutes.

In the inner pot, place the Air Fryer basket.

Close the Crisp Lid and press the "Broil" setting. Set temperature to 400°F and set the timer to 6 minutes. Press "Start."

Halfway down, open the Crisp Lid, flip the patties, and close the lid to continue cooking for the remaining time.

Open the Crisp Lid after cooking time is over. Serve warm with your choice of dip or ketchup.

Dinner

Rosemary Veggie Gratin

Preparation Time: 10 minutes

Cooking Time: 20 minutes

Servings: 4

Ingredients:

¾ pound cauliflower, steamed

1 onion, sliced

2 garlic cloves, minced

1 bell pepper, deveined

2 eggs, whipped

1 cup cream

Salt and pepper to taste

1 teaspoon cayenne pepper

1 tablespoon fresh rosemary

Directions:

Preheat your Air Fryer to 325 degrees F

Place vegetables in a lightly greased casserole dish, add remaining ingredients and stir

Spoon cream on top

Transfer to Air Fryer and cook for 20 minutes

Serve and enjoy!

Vegan Sausages

Preparation Time: 15 minutes

Cooking Time: 20 minutes

Servings:4

Ingredients:

200 grams Brown Mushrooms

150 grams Walnuts

1 tbsp Miso Paste

1 tbsp Tomato Paste

75 grams Panko

1 tsp Paprika

1 tsp Dried Sage

1 tsp Salt

½ tsp Black Pepper

Directions:

Blend all ingredients in a food processor.

Divide mixture into serving-sized portions and shape into sausages.

Coat the frying basket with non-stick spray and cook for 20 minutes at 370F, flipping halfway.

Spicy Short Ribs in Red Wine Reduction

Preparation Time: 3 hrs.

Cooking Time: 20 minutes

Servings: 6

Ingredients:

1 ½ pounds short ribs,

1 cup red wine

1/2 cup tamari sauce

1 lemon, juiced

1 teaspoon fresh ginger, grated

1 teaspoon salt

1 teaspoon black pepper

1 teaspoon paprika

1 teaspoon chipotle chili powder,

1 cup ketchup

1 teaspoon garlic powder,

1 teaspoon cumin

Directions:

In a ceramic bowl, place the beef ribs, wine, tamari sauce, lemon juice, ginger, salt, black pepper, paprika, and chipotle chili powder. Cover and let it marinate for 3 hours in the refrigerator. Discard the marinade and add the short ribs to the air fryer basket. Cook in the preheated air fry at 380 degrees f for 10 minutes, turning them over halfway through the cooking time. In the meantime, heat the saucepan over medium heat; add the reserved marinade and stir in the ketchup, garlic powder, and cumin. Cook until the sauce has thickened slightly. Pour the sauce over the warm ribs and serve immediately. Bon appétit!

Coffee Rubbed Steaks

Preparation Time: 10 minutes

Cooking Time: 15 minutes

Servings: 4

Ingredients:

1 and ½ tablespoons coffee, ground

4 rib eye steaks

½ tablespoon sweet paprika

2 tablespoons chili powder

2 teaspoons garlic powder

2 teaspoons onion powder

¼ teaspoon ginger, ground

¼ teaspoon, coriander, ground

A pinch of cayenne pepper

Black pepper to the taste

Directions:

In a bowl, mix coffee with paprika, chili powder, garlic powder, onion powder, ginger, coriander, cayenne and black pepper, stir, rub steaks with this mix, put in preheated air fryer and cook at 360 degrees F for 15 minutes.

Divide steaks on plates and serve with a side salad. Enjoy!

Creamy Cajun Chicken

Preparation Time: 30 minutes

Cooking Time: 20 minutes

Servings: 6

Ingredients:

3 green onions, thinly sliced

½ tablespoon Cajun seasoning

1 ½ cup buttermilk

2 large-sized chicken breasts, cut into strips

1/2 teaspoon garlic powder

1 teaspoon salt

1 cup cornmeal mix

1 teaspoon shallot powder

1 ½ cup flour

1 teaspoon ground black pepper, or to taste

Directions:

Prepare three mixing bowls. Combine 1/2 cup of the plain flour together with the cornmeal and Cajun seasoning in your bowl. In another bowl, place the buttermilk.

Pour the remaining 1 cup of flour into the third bowl.

Sprinkle the chicken strips with all the seasonings. Then, dip each chicken strip in the 1 cup of flour, then in the buttermilk; finally, dredge them in the cornmeal mixture.

Cook the chicken strips in the air fryer baking pan for 16 minutes at 365 degrees F. Serve garnished with green onions. Bon appétit!

Turkey with Mushrooms and Peas Casserole

Preparation Time: 20 minutes

Cooking Time: 30 minutes

Servings: 4

Ingredients:

chopped yellow onion 1

Salt and black pepper to the taste

chopped celery stalk; -1

skinless, boneless turkey breasts-2 lbs.

peas 1/2 cup

cream of mushrooms soup-1 cup

chicken stock-1 cup

bread cubes-1 cup

Directions:

Mix turkey with salt, pepper, onion, celery, peas, and stock in a dish that accommodates your air fryer

Introduce blend in your air fryer and cook at 360 °F, for 15 minutes.

Include bread solid shapes and cream of mushroom soup; mix, hurl and cook at 360 °F, for 5 minutes more.

Share the supper among plates and serve hot.

Thyme Chicken Balls

Preparation Time: 10 minutes

Cooking Time: 10 minutes

Servings: 4

Ingredients:

1-lb. ground chicken

1/3 cup panko

1 teaspoon salt

2 teaspoons chives

1/2 teaspoon garlic powder

1 teaspoon thyme

1 egg

Directions:

Toss all the meatball ingredients in a bowl and mix well.

Make small meatballs out this mixture and place them in the air fryer basket.

Press "Power Button" of Air Fry Oven and turn the dial to select the "Air Fry" mode.

Press the Time button and again turn the dial to set the cooking time to 10 minutes.

Now push the Temp button and rotate the dial to set the temperature at 350 degrees F.

Once preheated, place the air fryer basket inside and close its lid.

Serve warm

Ranch Fish Fillet

Preparation Time: 10 minutes

Cooking Time: 12 minutes

Servings: 4

Ingredients:

4 tilapia or salmon fillets

¾ cup bread crumbs

1 ounce ranch style dressing mix, dry

2½ tablespoons cooking oil

2 eggs

Lemon wedges – 1 lemon

Directions:

In a medium bowl beat eggs and keep it aside.

Combine ranch dressing and breadcrumbs in a medium bowl.

Pour cooking oil into it and stir until it becomes loose.

Set the air temperature to 180 degrees Celsius and preheat the air fryer.

Now start the cooking process.

Dip the fish fillet into the beaten egg and let to drip off the excess liquid.

Dredge the fish fillet into the crumb mixture.

Place the coated fish fillet into the air fryer.

Cook for 12 minutes.

Serve along with lemon wedges.

Herbed Fish Fingers

Preparation Time: 30 minutes

Cooking Time: 30 minutes

Servings: 4

Ingredients:

10½ ounces seer fish

½ teaspoon red chili flakes

¼ teaspoon turmeric powder

 2 teaspoons garlic powder

 1 teaspoon ginger paste

½ teaspoon black pepper, crushed

 2 teaspoons mixed herbs, powdered

 2 tablespoons corn flour

 2 eggs

¼ teaspoon baking soda

 1 cup breadcrumbs

Cooking spray – as required

2 tablespoons lemon juice

½ teaspoon salt

Directions:

Wash, clean and cut seer fish into a finger shape. Pat dry and keep it aside.

Combine thoroughly lemon juice, turmeric powder, red chili flakes, crushed black pepper, 1 teaspoon garlic powder, ginger paste, 1 teaspoon mixed herbs and salt in a medium bowl.

Put seer fish fingers into it and gently combine to marinate. Keep it aside for 10 minutes.

In another medium bowl, beat eggs and add corn flour.

Dip the marinated fish into it and keep aside for 10 minutes.

Take another bowl and mix breadcrumbs, 1 teaspoon mixed herbs and one teaspoon garlic powder.

Dredge the fish into the flour mixture.

Set the air fryer temperature to 180 degrees Celsius.

Place an aluminum liner inside of the air fryer basket.

Layer the marinated fish inside the air fryer basket without overlapping one another.

Spritz cooking oil over the fish.

Cook for 10 minutes by flipping half way.

Serve hot along with your favorite sauce.

Quick and Easy Lobster Tails

Preparation Time: 5 minutes

Cooking Time: 6 minutes

Servings: 2

Ingredients:

 4 lobster tails

 2 tablespoons melted butter

 1 teaspoon ground pepper

½ teaspoon salt

Directions:

Cut the lobster lengthwise.

Remove the shells and devein.

Coat the lobster with melted butter, pepper, and salt.

Set the air fryer temperature at 180 degrees Celsius and preheat.

Put the coated lobster in the air fryer basket and cook for 6 minutes.

Shake the air basket intermittently and sprinkle the remaining butter over it and continue cooking until it becomes crisp.

Serve hot.

Desserts

Fruit Custard

Preparation Time: 10 minutes

Cooking Time: 10 minutes

Servings: 2

Ingredients:

1 cup mixed fruits

2 cups milk

2 tbsp. custard powder

3 tbsp. powdered sugar

3 tbsp. unsalted butter

Directions:

Heat the milk and sugar and add the custard powder, then fruit and mix till you get a thick blend.

Preheat the air fryer to 300 F for 5 minutes.

Place the dish in the container and lower the temperature to 250 F. Cook for ten minutes and set aside to cool.

Beet Root Pudding

Preparation Time: 15 minutes

Cooking Time: 10 minutes

Servings: 6

Ingredients:

18 almonds, peeled

One teaspoon of cardamom powder

½ cup of condensed milk

1-pound of green beetroot, freshly grated

Two tablespoons of unsalted butter

Three tablespoons of mascarpone cheese

Three tablespoons of whipped cream

½ cup full-fat milk

Direction:

Set the Air fryer to 350 degrees F for 35 minutes. Combine beetroot with all the other ingredients in a bowl except cream and almonds. Pour this beetroot mixture into a baking dish. Place the baking dish on the cooking tray. Insert the cooking tray in the Air fryer when it displays "Add Food." Remove from the oven when cooking time is complete. Top the pudding with almonds and whipped cream to serve.

Lemon Poppy Muffins

Preparation Time: 15 minutes

Cooking Time: 15 minutes

Servings: 8

Ingredients:

2 cups All-purpose flour

1 ½ cup milk

½ tsp. baking powder

½ tsp. baking soda

2 tbsp. butter

1 tbsp. sugar

2 tbsp. lemon juice

2 tsp. vinegar

1 tbsp. crushed poppy seeds

Muffin cups

Directions:

Combine the ingredients except milk to create a crumbly blend.

Add this milk to the blend and make a batter and pour into the muffin cups.

Preheat the fryer to 300 F and cook 15 minutes.

Check whether they are done using a toothpick.

Caramel Muffins

Preparation Time: 10 minutes

Cooking Time: 12 minutes

Servings: 2

Ingredients:

 1 oz caramel

1 egg

4 oz sour cream

1/3 teaspoon baking powder

4 tablespoon flour

2 teaspoon white sugar

1 teaspoon butter

Directions:

Beat the egg in the mixing bowl and whisk it.

Add sour cream and baking powder.

After this, add flour, white sugar, and butter.

Use the mixer to make the smooth mass.

Then pour the dough into the muffin molds.

Fill the piping bag with the caramel.

Fill the muffin dough with the caramel.

Preheat the air fryer to 365 F.

Place the muffins in the air fryer basket and cook them for 12 minutes.

Cinnamon Churros

Preparation Time: 10 minutes

Cooking Time: 6 minutes

Servings: 2

Ingredients:

¼ cup water, hot

1 egg

1 pinch salt

1/3 cup flour

1 tablespoon butter

1 tablespoon brown sugar

1 teaspoon ground cinnamon

Directions:

Combine together flour, butter, salt, and hot water.

Mix the mixture until smooth.

Then beat the egg in the flour mixture and mix it with the help of the hand mixer.

Fill the piping bag with the dough.

Cover the air fryer basket with the parchment.

Make the small sticks (churros) from the dough.

Preheat the air fryer to 400 F and cook the meal for 6 minutes.

Meanwhile, combine together the brown sugar and ground cinnamon.

Toss the cooked churros to the sugar mixture and coat well.

Serve the dessert and enjoy!

Chocolate Oatmeal Cookies

Preparation Time: 10 minutes

Cooking Time: 7 minutes

Servings: 2

Ingredients:

1 tablespoon chocolate chips

3 tablespoon flour

3 tablespoon butter

1 tablespoon oatmeal

1 teaspoon lemon zest

¼ teaspoon vanilla sugar

Directions:

Melt the butter and combine it together with the chocolate chips and flour.

Add oatmeal, lemon zest, and vanilla sugar.

Mix the mixture carefully with the help of the spoon and then knead it with the help of the fingertips.

Make the medium balls from the dough and flatten them gently in the shape of the cookies.

Preheat the air fryer to 365 F.

Place the cookies in the air fryer basket and cook for 7 minutes. The time of cooking depends on the size of the cookies.

When the cookies are cooked – let them chill well and serve.

Cashew Cookies

Preparation Time: 15 minutes

Cooking Time: 15 minutes

Servings: 2

Ingredients:

 3 tablespoon flour

1 teaspoon butter

1 teaspoon cashew, crushed

½ teaspoon vanilla extract

1 tablespoon brown sugar

½ teaspoon cream

Directions:

Make the butter soft and place it in the big bowl.

Add flour and vanilla extract.

After this, add brown sugar and cream.

Knead the smooth and non-sticky dough.

Roll the dough and make the cookies with the help of the cutter.

Sprinkle every cookie with the crushed cashews.

Press the surface of the cookies lightly.

Preheat the air fryer to 360 F.

Put the cookies in the air fryer basket tray and cook the cookies for 15 minutes.

When the cookies are cooked – let them chill briefly.

Pears and Espresso Cream

Preparation Time: 10 minutes

Cooking Time: 30 minutes

Servings: 4

Ingredients:

4 pears, halved and cored

2 tablespoons lemon juice

1 tablespoon sugar

2 tablespoons water

2 tablespoons butter

For the cream:

1 cup whipping cream

1 cup mascarpone

1/3 cup sugar

2 tablespoons espresso, cold

Directions:

In a bowl, mix pears halves with lemon juice, 1 tablespoons sugar, butter and water, toss well, transfer them to your air fryer and cook at 360 degrees F for 30 minutes.

Meanwhile, in a bowl, mix whipping cream with mascarpone, 1/3 cup sugar and espresso, whisk really well and keep in the fridge until pears are done.

Divide pears on plates, top with espresso cream and serve them.

Enjoy!

Blackberry Cream Cheese Mousse

Preparation Time: 15 minutes

Cooking Time: 6 minutes

Servings: 4

Ingredients:

1 teaspoon vanilla extract

½ cup cream cheese

½ cup almond milk

¼ cup blackberries

2 teaspoon stevia extract

2 tablespoon butter

¼ teaspoon cinnamon

Directions:

Preheat the air fryer to 320 F.

 Combine butter, vanilla extract, and almond milk and transfer the mixture to the air fryer.

Cook the mixture for 6 minutes or well combined.

Then stir it carefully and chill to room temperature.

Crush the blackberries.

Whisk the cream cheese using a hand whisker for 2 minutes.

Add the crushed blackberries and whisk for 1 minute more.

Add cinnamon and stevia extract.

Stir gently.

Combine the almond butter liquid and cream cheese mixture together.

Mix using a hand mixer.

When well mixed pour into a glass vessel.

Place it in the fridge and cool.

Hazelnut Spread

Preparation Time: 10 minutes

Cooking Time: 6 minutes

Servings: 4

Ingredients:

1 oz. dark chocolate

3 oz. hazelnuts, crushed

4 tablespoon butter

¼ cup almond milk

½ teaspoon vanilla extract

1 teaspoon stevia

Directions:

Preheat the air fryer to 360 F.

Put the dark chocolate, crushed hazelnuts, butter, almond milk, vanilla extract, and stevia in the air fryer basket.

Mix well and cook for 2 minutes.

Mix again with a hand mixer.

Cook the mixture for 1 minute.

Stir the mixture again and pour it into a glass vessel.

Put the mixture in the fridge and let it cool until it is solid.

Conclusion

Unlike frying things in a typical pan on gas which fails to make your fries crisp and leaves your samosa uncooked due to uneven heat. The inbuilt kitchen deep fryers do it all; you can have perfectly crisp French fries like the one you get in restaurants. Your samosas will be perfectly cooked inside-out. Well, the list doesn't end here it goes on and on the potato wedges, chicken and much more. You can make many starters and dishes using fryer and relish the taste buds of your loved ones.

The new air fryers come along with a lot of features, so you don't mess up doing things enjoy your cooking experience. The free hot to set the temperature according to your convenience both mechanically and electronically. Oil filters to reuse the oil and use it for a long run. With the ventilation system to reduce and eliminate the frying odor. In a few models you also get the automatic timers and alarm set for convenient cooking, frying I mean. Also, the auto- push and raise feature to immerse or hold back the frying basket to achieve the perfect frying aim.

Thank you for purchasing this cookbook I hope you will apply all the acquired knowledge productively.

<u>Notes:</u>

Lightning Source UK Ltd.
Milton Keynes UK
UKHW020808080621
385129UK00001B/140